Seeli and Huddlig
This is my
FAVORITE Christmas
book!!!

NEVER FORGET:

God has a special
place for you when
you feel left out.

Miss Lori

The CRIPPLED LAMB

MAX LUCADO

with JENNA, ANDREA, & SARA LUCADO

illustrated by Liz Bonham

A Division of Thomas Nelson Publishers

NASHVILLE   DALLAS   MEXICO CITY   RIO DE JANEIRO

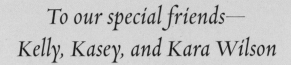

To our special friends—
Kelly, Kasey, and Kara Wilson

The Crippled Lamb
Text © 1994, 1999 by Max Lucado
Illustration © 1994, 1999 by Liz Bonham
Karen Hill, executive editor to Max Lucado

Published in Nashville, Tennessee, by Tommy Nelson. Tommy Nelson is a registered trademark of Thomas Nelson, Inc.

Tommy Nelson® titles may be purchased in bulk for educational, business, fund-raising, or sales promotional use. For information, please e-mail SpecialMarkets@ThomasNelson.com.

ISBN 978-1-4003-1807-0 (2011 7x9 edition)

The Library of Congress has cataloged the earlier printing as follows:

Lucado, Max
    The crippled lamb/ by Max Lucado with Jenna, Andrea, & Sara Lucado;
Illustrations by Liz Bonham.
        p. cm.
    Summary: A lamb who has always felt different and sad because of his black spots and his limp, feels his true worth when he is called upon to help keep the baby Jesus warm.
    ISBN 0-8499-1005-6, ISBN 0-8499-5979-9 (5th Anniversary)
    [1. Sheep—Fiction. 2. Jesus Christ—Nativity—Fiction.]
I. Bonham, Liz, ill. II. Title.
PZ7.L9684Cr 1994
[E]-dc20

94-19865
CIP
AC

21 22 EP 20 19 18 17 16 / Printed in Spain by Estellaprint /

Dear Friend,

Returning to a familiar story is like revisiting an old friend . . . inviting, comfortable. If you're renewing your acquaintance with The Crippled Lamb, we hope you feel just that way—as if you've rediscovered an old friend. If you're new to the story, we pray its message will bless your life.

We're grateful to God for placing this story on our hearts so we could share it with you. The message is a simple, but precious reminder: God's love extends to all, and he has a special place for each of his children.

May you always remember how much he loves you.

Warmly,

Max Lucado
Jenna, Andrea, and Sara

Once upon a time in a sunny valley, there lived a little lamb named Joshua. He was white with black spots, black feet, and . . . sad eyes.

Josh felt sad when he saw the other lambs with snow-white wool and no spots. He felt sad when he saw the other sheep with their moms and dads because he didn't have a mom or dad.

But he felt saddest when he saw the other lambs running and jumping, because he couldn't. Josh had been born with one leg that didn't work right. He was crippled. He always limped when he walked.

That's why he always watched while the other lambs ran and played. Josh felt sad and alone—except when Abigail was around.

Abigail was Josh's best friend. She didn't look like a friend for a lamb. She was an old cow. She was brown with white blotches that looked like rain puddles on a path. Her belly was as round as a barrel, and her voice was always kind and friendly.

Some of Josh's favorite hours were spent with Abigail.

They loved to pretend they were on adventures in distant lands. Josh liked to listen to Abigail tell stories about the stars. They would spend hours on the hill, looking into the valley. They were good friends.

But even with a friend like Abigail, Josh still got sad. It made him sad to be the only lamb who could not run and jump and play in the grass. That's when Abigail would turn to him and say, "Don't be sad, little Joshua. God has a special place for those who feel left out."

Josh wanted to believe her. But it was hard. Some days he just felt alone. He really felt alone the day the shepherds decided to take the lambs to the next valley where there was more grass. The sheep had been in this valley so long, the ground was nearly bare.

All the sheep were excited when the shepherd told them they were going to a new meadow.

As they prepared to leave, Josh hobbled over and took his place on the edge of the group. But the others started laughing at him.

"You're too slow to go all the way to the next valley."

"Go back, Slowpoke. We'll never get there if we have to wait on you!"

"Go back, Joshua."

That's when Josh looked up and saw the shepherd
standing in front of him. "They are right, my little Joshua.
You better go back. This trip is too long for you. Go and
spend the night in the stable."

Josh looked at the man for a long time. Then he turned
slowly and began limping away.

When Josh got to the top of the hill, he looked down and saw all the other sheep headed toward the green grass. Never before had he felt so left out. A big tear slipped out of his eye, rolled down his nose, and fell on a rock.

Just then he heard Abigail behind him. And Abigail said what she always said when Josh felt sad. "Don't be sad, little Joshua. God has a special place for those who feel left out."

Slowly the two friends turned and walked to the stable together.

By the time they got to the little barn, the sun was setting like a big orange ball. Josh and Abigail went inside and began to eat some hay out of the feed box. They were very hungry, and the hay tasted good. For a little while, Joshua forgot that he had been left behind.

"Go to sleep, little friend," Abigail said after they finished eating. "You've had a hard day."

Josh was tired. So he lay down in the corner on some straw and closed his eyes. He felt Abigail lie down beside him, and he was glad to have Abigail as a friend.

Soon Josh was asleep. At first, he slept soundly, curled up against Abigail's back. In his sleep he dreamed. He dreamed of running and jumping just like the other sheep. He dreamed of long walks with Abigail through the valley. He dreamed of being in a place where he never felt left out.

Suddenly strange noises woke him up.

"Abigail," he whispered, "wake up. I'm scared."

Abigail lifted her big head and looked around. The stable was dark except for a small lamp hanging on the wall.

"Somebody is in here," Josh whispered.

They looked across the dimly lighted stable. There, lying on some fresh hay in the feed box, was a baby. A young woman was resting on a big pile of hay beside the feed box.

Joshua looked at Abigail, thinking his friend could tell him what was going on. But Abigail was just as surprised as Josh.

Josh looked again at the woman and the child, then limped across the stable. He stopped next to the mother and looked into the baby's face. The baby was crying. He was cold. The woman picked up the baby and put him on the hay next to her.

Josh looked around the stable for something to keep the baby warm. Usually there were blankets. But not tonight. The shepherds had taken them on their trip across the valley.

Then Josh remembered his own soft, warm wool. Timidly, he walked over and curled up close to the baby.

"Thank you, little lamb," the baby's mother said softly.

Soon the little child stopped crying and went back to sleep.

About that time, a man entered the stable carrying some rags.

"I'm sorry, Mary," he explained. "This is all the cover I could find."

"It's okay," she answered. "This little lamb has kept the new king warm."

A king? Joshua looked at the baby and wondered who he might be.

"His name is Jesus." Mary spoke as if she knew Josh's question. "God's Son. He came from heaven to teach us about God."

Just then there was another noise at the door. It was the shepherds—the ones who had left Joshua behind. Their eyes were big, and they were excited.

"We saw a bright light and heard the angels . . ." they began. Then they saw Joshua next to the baby.

"Joshua! Do you know who this baby is?"

"He does now." It was the young mother who was speaking. She looked at Joshua and smiled. "God has heard your prayers, little lamb. This little baby is the answer."

Joshua looked down at the baby. Somehow he knew this was a special child, and this was a special moment.

He also understood why he had been born with a crippled leg. Had he been like the other sheep, he would have been in the valley. But since he was different, he was in the stable, among the first to welcome Jesus into the world.

Joshua turned and walked back to Abigail and took his place beside his friend. "You were right," he told her. "God does have a special place for me."